Sagrario Salaberri • Aaron Jolly
Series advisor: David Nunan

Pearson Education Limited
Edinburgh Gate
Harlow
Essex CM20 2JE
England
and Associated Companies throughout the world.

Poptropica English

© Pearson Education Limited 2015

Based on the work of Sagrario Salaberri

The rights of Sagrario Salaberri, and Aaron Jolly to be identified as authors of this work have been asserted by them in accordance with the Copyright, Designs and Patents Act 1988.

Stories on pages 6–7, 16, 28, 40, 52, 64, 76, 88, and 100 by Hawys Morgan. The rights of Hawys Morgan to be identified as authors of this work have been asserted by them in accordance with the Copyright, Designs and Patents Act 1988.

Phonics syllabus and activities by Rachel Wilson

Editorial and project management by hyphen

All rights reserved; no part of this publication may be reproduced, stored in a retrieval system, or transmitted in any form or by any means, electronic, mechanical, photocopying, recording, or otherwise without the prior written permission of the Publishers.

First published 2015

ISBN: 978-1-292-39252-3

Set in Fiendstar 15/24pt

Printed in Slovakia by Neografia

Illustrators: Humberto Blanco (Sylvie Poggio Artists Agency), Anja Boretzki (Good Illustration), Martyn Cain (Beehive Illustration), Chan Cho Fai, Lee Cosgrove, Leo Cultura, Nigel Dobbyn (Beehive Ilustration), Bill Greenhead (Illustration), Marek Jagucki, Mark Ruffle (The Organisation), Anjan Sarkar (Good Illustration), Dickie Seto and Olimpia Wong

Picture Credits: The publisher would like to thank the following for their kind permission to reproduce their photographs:

(Key: b–bottom; c–centre; l–left; r–right; t–top)

123RF.com: 22br, 34cr, 47tr, 62tc/2, 68tr, 75bl, Arvind Balaraman 63cr, Jacek Chabraszewski 15r, dmbaker 23t, Peter Dojkic 23cr, Duncan Drummond 18l, Lajos Endrédi 78bl, Robert Findlay 74tr, Andrey Golubev 102/4, Eric Isselee 26tr/2, Kelly Kane 54bl, Cathy Keifer 78br, Markus Mainka 14c/2, Oleg Mikhaylov 14tl, Sergey Novikov 70tc, Anna Omelchenko 47tl, 71tc, rustyphil 30cl, Michael Sheehan 35br, Johan Swanepoel 30tr, Mr.Thuvthongchai Uysa 26cr/2, Anna Yakimova 70bc, Lisa Young 34bl; **Alamy Images:** Bill Bachman 54br, Eyebyte 94bl, F. Jack Jackson 46tr, Juniors Bildarchiv GmbH 27bl, Michael Matthews 95, OJO Images Ltd 68cl, Rubberball 62c/2, Bettina Strenske 94tc, Travelscape Images 94cr; **Bahamas Tourist Office:** 63tl, 99br; **Corbis:** Lucidio Studio Inc. 42t, Moodboard 22tr; **Creatas:** Thinkstock 14cr; **Fotolia.com:** Jacek Chabraszewski 14tc/1, Petro Feketa 34br, Junial Enterprises 18r, A. Karnholz 42c, Ivan Kmit 38, krasnevsky 26cl, .shock 62tc/1, SolisImages 62c/1, 68c/2, Sandra Zuerlein 15l; **Getty Images:** Alistair Berg 22cl, Hiroyuki Ito 70br, Kail Nine LLC 27br, Mike Marsland 71cr, Jason Merritt 9cr, National Basketball Association 70cl, Stuart C Wilson 9cl, WireImage / Kevin Mazur 9cr/2; **Imagemore Co., Ltd:** 26tl; **Pearson Education Ltd:** Jon Barlow 15bl, 46cl, 66tl, 87, 107bl, Sophie Bluy 59tr, Gareth Boden 111, Trevor Clifford 49bc, 49br, Jules Selmes 14tr, Studio 8 14c/1; **PhotoDisc:** 18cr, 26tl/2, Jack Hollingsworth Photography 35bc, Photolink 75cl, John Rowley 62tl, StockTrek 42tr; **Shutterstock.com:** 70sphotography 94tl, AGIF 71tl, Angela Kay Agnew 46cr, Ammit Jack 98tl, Aspen Photo 14tc/2, Joe Belanger 102bl, Mircea Bezergheanu 102br, Mark Bonham 68tl, Pawe Borowka 102tr, Rich Carey 46tl, 102cl, Diego Cervo 98tr, Chesapeake 78tr, Cozyta 68tc/2, Debbie Aird Photography 30cr, Jaimie Duplass 107cl, Helga Esteb 9c, Vladislav Gajiic 102/2, Xavier Gallego Morell 34cl, Andrzej Gibasiewicz 74tc/2, Golden Pixels LLC. 15br, GuoZhongHua 66cl, Ruslan Guzov 94bc, hektoR 98tc, iofoto 59bl, Eric Isselee 26tr, Ivalin 74tl, Roger Jegg – Fotodesign-Jegg.de 59tl, Jenkedco 18c, John Roman Images 68c/1, KateStone 63c/1, Henrik Lehnerer 78c, Magicoven 66tr, Stephen Mcsweeney 62cr, Monkey Business Images 14cl, 15c, 59br, 63tr, Natursports 102bc, Vitalii Nesterchuk 98tl/2, Ocean Image Photography 98tr/2, Pete Pahham 71c, pandapaw 26tc, Pressmaster 68tc/1, ra2studio 62cl, Raxpixel 54bc, s_bukley 9cl/2, SergiyN 99t, Slaven 62tr, Pal Teravagimov 75br, The Whiteview 26cr, Andrey Yurlov 74tc/1, Oleg Znamensky 26c; **Sozaijiten:** 68cr; **www.imagesource.com:** 26cl/2

All other images © Pearson Education

Every effort has been made to trace the copyright holders and we apologize in advance for any unintentional omissions. We would be pleased to insert the appropriate acknowledgement in any subsequent edition of this publication.

Scope and sequence 4
Welcome 6
1 Free time 12
Wider World 1 22
2 Wild animals 24
Review Units 1 and 2 34
3 The seasons 36
Wider World 2 46
4 My week 48
Review Units 3 and 4 58
5 Jobs 60
Wider World 3 70
6 In the rain forest 72
Review Units 5 and 6 82
7 Feelings 84
Wider World 4 94
8 By the sea 96
Review Units 7 and 8 106
Goodbye 108
Festivals 112
Wordlist 116

Scope and sequence

Welcome

Vocabulary:	**Adjectives:** funny, smart, shy, kind, quiet
Structures:	I'm taller than Sophie/you/him/her. He's/She's taller than Sophie/you/me. You're taller than Sophie/me/him/her. My hands are bigger.

1 Free time

Vocabulary:	**Leisure activities:** cooking, playing the guitar, chatting online, playing video games, skateboarding, watching TV, skiing, skipping, painting, playing hockey, reading magazines, watching movies, surfing the Internet, walking the dog, riding a scooter	**Values:** Set goals. **Cross-curricular:** **Social science:** Places to live **Phonics: ou, ow** cloud, snow
Structures:	What do you/they like doing? I/We/They like skiing. What does he/she like doing? He/She likes skiing. I/We/They don't like skiing. He/She doesn't like skiing. Do you/they like skipping? Yes, I/they do. / No, I/they don't. Does he/she like skipping? Yes, he/she does. / No, he/she doesn't.	

2 Wild animals

Vocabulary:	**Wild animals:** giraffe, lion, elephant, crocodile, hippo, monkey, crab, camel, zebra, panda, gorilla **Food:** grass, leaves **Habitats:** river, desert, grassland, forest, rain forest	**Values:** Protect wildlife. **Cross-curricular:** **Science:** Elephants and giraffes **Phonics: all, aw** call, draw
Structures:	Giraffes eat leaves. Do giraffes eat leaves? Yes, they do. Do giraffes eat meat? No, they don't. What do crabs eat? They eat worms. Where do crabs live? They live in rivers.	

3 The seasons

Vocabulary:	**Weather:** stormy, lightning, thunder, humid, wet, temperature, degrees **Activities:** go camping, go water skiing, go hiking, go snowboarding **Seasons:** spring, summer, fall, winter	**Values:** Be a good friend. **Cross-curricular:** **Science:** Hurricanes **Phonics: ew, y** new, fly
Structures:	What's the weather like today? It's wet. / There's lightning and thunder. What's the temperature today? It's 25 degrees. I/We/They go camping in the spring. He/She goes camping in the spring.	

4 My week

Vocabulary:	**Activities:** practice the violin, study math, have music lessons, study English, practice the piano, have ballet lessons, learn to draw, learn to cook, do gymnastics, do karate **Time:** morning, noon, afternoon, evening, 2:15, quarter after two, 2:30, two-thirty, 2:45, quarter to three	**Values:** Try new things. **Cross-curricular:** **Social science:** Ways to go to school **Phonics: ie, ue** pie, blue
Structures:	What do you do on Saturday? I have music lessons on Saturday. / I have music lessons at two o'clock. What does he/she do on Saturday? He/She has music lessons on Saturday. / He/She has music lessons at two o'clock. When do you have music lessons? I have music lessons in the morning. / I have music lessons at 2:15/quarter after two. When does he/she have music lessons? He/She has music lessons in the morning. / He/She has music lessons at 2:15/quarter after two.	

5 Jobs

Vocabulary:	**Occupations:** an astronaut, a mechanic, a builder, a firefighter, a basketball player, a police officer, a ballet dancer, a movie star, a photographer, a singer, a model, a journalist, a fashion designer, a carpenter, a computer programmer, a lawyer, an athlete		**Values:** Study, do your chores, and have fun!
Structures:	What do you want to be? I want to be a builder/an astronaut. What does he/she want to be? He/She wants to be a builder/an astronaut. I don't want to be a builder/an astronaut. He/She doesn't want to be a builder/an astronaut. Do you want to be a singer? Yes, I do. / No, I don't. Does he/she want to be a singer? Yes, he/she does. / No, he/she doesn't.		**Cross-curricular:** **Social science:** Dreams and aspirations **Phonics: le, y** jungle, happy

6 In the rain forest

Vocabulary:	**Nature:** path, river, valley, bridge, mountain, waterfall, hut, cave, lake, sea, coast, hills **Prepositions:** around, through, toward, past		**Values:** Be prepared.
Structures:	Where is/are the hut/huts? It's/They're over the mountain. It's/They're across the bridge. It's/They're near the waterfall. It's/They're between the mountain and the river. Could you walk around the lake? Yes, I could. / No, I couldn't. I could walk around the lake, but I couldn't swim through it.		**Cross-curricular:** **Geography:** The Amazon rain forest **Phonics: ce, ce, ci, cir** center, ice, city, circus

7 Feelings

Vocabulary:	**Actions:** smiling, shaking, frowning, shouting, crying, laughing, blushing, yawning **Emotions:** nervous, proud, relieved, surprised, relaxed, embarrassed, worried		**Values:** Help others in need.
Structures:	Why are you crying? I'm crying because I'm sad. Why is he/she crying? He's/She's crying because he's/she's sad. What's the matter? I'm nervous. How do you feel? I feel nervous. What makes you feel nervous? Tests make me feel nervous.		**Cross-curricular:** **Social science:** Music and movies **Phonics: ge, dge** gem, page, bridge

8 By the sea

Vocabulary:	**Outdoor activities:** fishing, surfing, snorkeling, sailing, kayaking, horseback riding **Equipment:** a fishing pole, a surfboard, a life jacket, a snorkel, a paddle, riding boots **Emotions:** fond of, crazy about, bored with, scared of, terrified of **Extreme sports:** rafting, bungee jumping, rock climbing, scuba diving, hang gliding		**Values:** Enjoy all your activities.
Structures:	Let's go snorkeling/kayaking! Great idea! I love snorkeling. Sorry, I don't like kayaking. Do you have a snorkel/a paddle? Yes, I do. / No, I don't. What are you crazy about? I'm crazy about rafting.		**Cross-curricular:** **Science:** Coral reefs **Phonics: ph, wh** phone, white

1 🎧 Talk about the pictures. Then listen and read.

Lesson 1

Can understand a story

2 🎧 **Listen and read.**

3 🎧 **Listen. Write the names.**

1 _____ 2 _____ 3 _____ 4 _____

4 **Match.**

1 Sophie   a yellow scarf, brown coat, black shoes

2 Uncle James   b blue T-shirt, black shorts, green sneakers

3 Oliver   c red sweater, jeans, blue sneakers

4 Finley Keen   d yellow T-shirt, blue skirt, pink sneakers

5 **Introduce yourself to the class.**

> Hi! My name's Ann. I'm 10, and I like soccer.

8 Lesson 2   Can introduce myself

6   Listen and chant.

Do you like movie stars?
Yes, I do. Yes, I do.
Do you like movie stars?
No, I don't. No, I don't.
Do you like Finley Keen?
Yes, I do. Yes, I do.
Do you like Finley Keen?
No, I don't. No, I don't.

7   Ask and answer.

1. Daniel Radcliffe

2. Miranda Cosgrove

3. Zac Efron

4. Robert Pattinson

5. Jennifer Lawrence

Do you like...?
Yes, I do.
No, I don't.
Sorry, I don't know him/her.

8 Write four names of movie stars. Do a survey.

like =   don't like = 😞   don't know him/her =

Movie star	Me	_____ (Friend 1)	_____ (Friend 2)	_____ (Friend 3)
1				
2				
3				
4				

Lesson 3 Can talk about movie stars I like and don't like

9 Listen and number.

shy

kind

funny

quiet

smart

10 Listen and ✓ or ✗.

1

2

3

4

11 Act and guess.

Are you shy? — No, I'm not.
Are you quiet? — Yes, I am.

Lesson 4

Can identify people's personality

12 Listen and say.

tall	taller
short	shorter
big	bigger
small	smaller
young	younger
old	older
fast	faster
smart	smarter
shy	shyer
quiet	quieter
funny	funnier

LOOK!

I'm **taller than** Sophie/you/him/her.
He's/She's **taller than** Sophie/you/me.
You're **taller than** Sophie/me/him/her.
My hands are **bigger**.

13 Work with a friend. Compare and write.

1

I'm _____ than him/her.

2

My hands are _____.
His/Her hands are _____.

3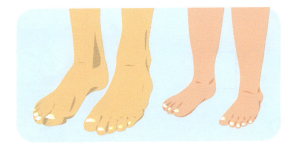

My feet are _____.
His/Her feet are _____.

4 How old are you?
I'm eight years and three months old.

I'm eight years and three months old.
I'm _____ than him/her.

Lesson 5

Can make comparisons

1 Free time

1 ⭐ What do you know?

2 🎧 Listen and find.

skateboarding
playing the guitar
cooking
chatting online
playing video games

3 🎧 Listen and write T = True or F = False.

4 🎧 Listen and say.

Lesson 1

Can identify free-time activities

5 Listen and chant.

Finley Keen... he's so cool.
He likes playing soccer,
He likes going to the pool.
Does he like skiing and watching TV?
Yes, he does, just like me!
Does he like cooking? Does he like cleaning?
No, he doesn't.
And he doesn't like reading.

LOOK!

What do you/they like doing?	I/We/They like skiing.
What does he/she like doing?	He/She likes skiing.

I/We/They don't like skiing. He/She doesn't like skiing.

6 Listen and ✓ or ✗.

1 What does Oliver like doing?
 a playing soccer ☐   b cooking ☐
 c chatting online ☐   d cleaning ☐

2 What does Sophie like doing?
 a skiing ☐   b reading ☐
 c watching TV ☐   d playing video games ☐

7 Ask and answer.

What do you like doing?   I like playing the guitar.

Lesson 2   Can ask and answer about what people like doing in their free time   **13**

8 Listen and number. Then say.

skipping

painting

playing hockey

reading magazines

watching movies

surfing the Internet

walking the dog

riding a scooter

9 Listen and circle. Then sing.

Do you like riding your (scooter / bike)?
Yes, I do. I like riding my (scooter / bike).
Do you like playing the (guitar / piano)?
Yes, I do. Look! Look! I'm a pop star.

What do you, do you like doing?
What do you, do you like doing?

Do you like playing (video games / soccer)?
No, I don't. I like riding my (scooter / bike).

Does your brother like (painting / skateboarding)?
Yes, he does. He likes (painting / skateboarding).

What does he, does he like doing?
What does he, does he like doing?

Lesson 3

Can identify more free-time activities

Do you/they **like skipping**?	**Yes**, I/they **do**.
	No, I/they **don't**.
Does he/she **like skipping**?	**Yes**, he/she **does**.
	No, he/she **doesn't**.

10 Listen, read, and stick. Then ask and answer.

This is my dog, Timmy. He doesn't like running, and he doesn't like catching a ball. But he likes skateboarding. Look! He's cool.

Hi, I'm Anna. I like singing with my friends. I don't like chatting online, but I like surfing the Internet.

I'm Charlie. I don't like watching TV. I like skiing. My sister doesn't like watching TV, either. She likes skiing with me. It's fun!

Does Timmy like running?

No, he doesn't. He likes skateboarding.

WRITING AND SPEAKING

11   Write. Then ask and answer.

I like _____.
I don't like _____.
My (mom, dad, brother, sister, or friend) likes _____.
_____ doesn't like _____.
_____.

Do you like chatting online?

Yes, I do.

Does your mom like watching TV?

No, she doesn't. She likes reading.

Lesson 4   Can ask and answer about what people like doing in their free time

12 Talk about the pictures. Then listen and read.

13 Role-play the story.

14 Circle.

1. Coco likes (riding a scooter / skateboarding).
2. Sophie loves (climbing / riding a scooter).
3. Sophie and Oliver are (faster / slower) than Coco.
4. Coco can (jump / ride a scooter).
5. Coco likes (skiing / climbing).

15 Check (✓) three goals. Then ask and answer.

VALUES
Set goals.

1. Me ☐ My friend ☐
Be a good son or daughter.

2. Me ☐ My friend ☐
Be a good student.

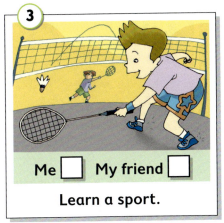
3. Me ☐ My friend ☐
Learn a sport.

4. Me ☐ My friend ☐
Learn to play an instrument.

5. Me ☐ My friend ☐
Make new friends.

6. Me ☐ My friend ☐
Help people.

I want to learn a new sport. What about you?

I want to be a good daughter.

Lesson 6 — Can understand details of a story / Can talk about setting goals

16   What do you know?

17   Listen and read. Then check (✓) and say.

Special houses

This is Rosa. Look at her house. It's a boat. Rosa likes her boat. She doesn't like watching TV. She likes reading and playing the guitar. She also likes riding her bike but not on the boat!

This is Will. This is his house. It's a lighthouse! Will likes living in the lighthouse, but he doesn't like climbing the stairs. He likes playing video games and watching TV. He likes cooking, too.

		Rosa	Will
1	likes reading	☐	☐
2	likes cooking	☐	☐
3	likes playing video games	☐	☐
4	doesn't like climbing the stairs	☐	☐
5	doesn't like watching TV	☐	☐

Rosa likes...
Will doesn't like...

Lesson 7 — Can understand a text about what other children like and don't like doing

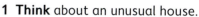 PROJECT 1

18 Design an unusual house.

1 **Think** about an unusual house.
2 **Draw** a picture of the house.
3 **Write** about things you can do in it.
4 **Share** your design with the class.

Tell your family about your unusual house. Show them your design.

PHONICS

19 Listen.

1  2

20 Listen and blend the sounds.

21 Underline *ou* and *ow*. Read the sentences aloud.

1 I can see a big rain cloud.

2 The yellow sun is low.

3 Blow the snow from the path.

4 Shout out loud!

Lesson 8   Can design an unusual house / Can pronounce the sounds *ou* and *ow*   19

22 **Listen and check (✓).**

1  a  b 2  a 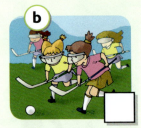 b

3  a  b 4  a  b

23 **Write.**

1  What does she like doing?
She _____ _____.

2  _____ _____?
He likes playing the guitar.

3  Do they like playing video games?
No, _____ _____.

4  Does she _____ _____?
Yes, she does!

24 **Choose a picture. Ask and answer.**

What does he like doing?   He likes cooking.

I can identify free-time activities.
I can ask and answer about what people like doing.
I can understand a text about what children like doing.

20 Lesson 9   Can assess what I have learned in Unit 1

25 Write. Then play.

HAVE FUN 1

	Family member 1 (man)	Family member 2 (woman)	Friend 1 (boy)	Friend 2 (girl)
Me				
My friend				

Friend 1. Does he like skateboarding?

No, he doesn't.

Does he like cooking?

No, he doesn't.

Does he like watching movies?

No, he doesn't. My turn.

1. Students work in pairs. Each student writes an activity for his/her family members and friends.

2. Students play rock-paper-scissors. The winner is the first one to ask about his/her classmate's family and friends. If he/she guesses correctly, he/she writes the name of the activity in the space provided.

3. Students take turns asking and answering. Each student is allowed to make three guesses. This is a timed activity – the student with more correct guesses when the time is over wins.

Now go to Poptropica English World

Lesson 10

Can use what I have learned in Unit 1

21

Wider World 1

On the weekend

1 What do you know?

2 Listen and read.

"Hi, I'm Kelly. I'm from Canada. It's snowy here. I like skiing. It's fun. I can go very fast. Do you like skiing?"

"Hi, I'm Tumelo. I'm from South Africa. I like playing soccer at school with my friends. I can see the Soccer City stadium from my house. It's really big. My favorite team is the Mamelodi Sundowns."

3 Listen and say the names.

Wider World 1 — Can understand texts about what other children like doing on the weekend

3

Hi, I'm Anne. I'm from France. I like riding my bike with my mom and dad. It's good exercise. I like riding my bike on sunny days. My little brother likes riding, too!

Hi, I'm Carlos. I'm from Mexico. Look! I'm at a beautiful water park in Cancun. I like swimming and floating down the stream with my friends. It's great!

4 **Write T = True or F = False.**

1   Kelly can't ski fast. ☐
2   Tumelo likes playing soccer at school. ☐
3   Anne likes riding her bike with her family. ☐
4   Carlos goes to the water park with his family. ☐

5 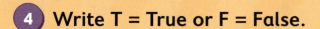 Ask your friend about his/her hobbies.

Do you like playing soccer?   Yes, I do.

Wider World 1   Can ask and answer about hobbies   23

2 Wild animals

1 ⭐ What do you know?

2 🎧 A:30 Listen and find.

- giraffe
- lion
- elephant
- crocodile
- grass

3 🎧 A:31 Listen and ✓ or ✗.

1.
2.
3.
5.
6.
7.

4 🎧 A:32 Listen and say.

24 Lesson 1 · Can identify wild animals and their food

5 Listen and chant.

Do hippos eat insects?
No, they don't. Hippos eat grass.
Do monkeys eat grass?
No, they don't. Monkeys eat fruit.
Do lions eat meat?
Yes, they do. Lions eat meat.
Do giraffes eat leaves?
Yes, they do. Giraffes eat leaves.

Giraffes eat leaves.

Do giraffes eat	leaves?	Yes, they do.
	meat?	No, they don't.

6 Write. Then listen and check your answers.

1   Lions eat _____.

2   Crocodiles eat _____.

3   Giraffes eat _____.

4   Hippos eat _____.

5   Elephants eat _____ and _____.

6   Monkeys eat _____.

7 Ask and answer.

Do hippos eat meat?

No, they don't.

Lesson 2

Can ask and answer about what wild animals eat   25

8 Listen and number. Then say.

VOCABULARY

| a crab | b camel | c zebra | d panda | e gorilla |
| f river | g desert | h grassland | i forest | j rain forest |

9 Listen and circle. Then sing.

SONG

(Zebras / Lions) live in (forests / grasslands).
They're big and strong.
They like sleeping all day long.
They run very fast to catch their lunch.
What do they eat? They eat (meat / leaves).
Crunch, crunch, munch!

(Pandas / Gorillas) live in (rain forests / forests).
They're big and cute.
They like eating all day long.
They climb tall trees to find their lunch.
What do they eat?
They eat (leaves / fruit).
Crunch, crunch, munch!

26 Lesson 3   Can identify more wild animals and where they live

10   **Draw and write. Then ask and answer.**

LOOK! A:40

What do crabs eat?	They eat worms.
Where do crabs live?	They live in rivers.

My favorite wild animal

I like _____.

They live in _____.

They eat _____.

- I like giraffes.
- Where do they live?
- They live in grasslands.
- Do they eat meat?
- No, they don't. They eat leaves.

11   **Listen and read. Then write.**

Discovery Island Animal Park: Crocodiles

Blog posted by: Paul, animal park keeper

Hi, I'm Paul. There are a lot of crocodiles here at Discovery Island Animal Park. This is Snapper. Look at the bird in her mouth! It's cleaning her teeth.

Crocodiles live in Africa and Australia. They live in rivers. They are very big and strong. They can swim very well. Crocodiles have very big mouths with 65 teeth. They eat meat and fish. They can eat you, too, so watch out!

1   What is the bird doing in Snapper's mouth?   _____

2   Where do crocodiles live?   _____

3   What do crocodiles eat?   _____

Lesson 4   Can ask and answer about wild animals   27

12 Talk about the pictures. Then listen and read.

13 Role-play the story.

14 Write the answers.

1 Do giraffes eat paper? _____

2 What do monkeys eat? _____

3 Is Uncle James scared of the gorilla? _____

4 Do gorillas eat bananas? _____

5 Do gorillas like fruit for lunch? _____

15 Check (✓) three things. Then ask and answer.

Protect wildlife.

1 Me ☐ My friend ☐
Give money.

2 Me ☐ My friend ☐
Join a nature club.

3 Me ☐ My friend ☐
Learn more about wildlife.

4 Me ☐ My friend ☐
Get my friends to help.

5 Me ☐ My friend ☐
Recycle.

6 Me ☐ My friend ☐
Do a school project.

I want to join a nature club. What about you?

I want to get my friends to help.

Lesson 6   Can understand details of a story / Can talk about ways to protect wildlife

16   What do you know?

17   Listen and read. Then write T = True or F = False.

Amazing Animals!

Elephants

Elephants live in grasslands and forests in Africa and India. They eat grass, leaves, fruit, and flowers. They can eat more than 300 kg a day. They only have four teeth, so they don't eat meat. Did you know that elephants can say hello with their trunks?

Giraffes

Giraffes also live in grasslands and forests of Africa. They eat leaves, fruit, flowers, and sometimes small trees. They don't drink every day. They can live for one week without water. They sleep standing up, but they don't sleep very much. They have long black tongues. Did you know that they can clean their ears with their tongues?

1 Elephants eat a lot. ☐

2 Elephants have a lot of teeth. ☐

3 Elephants say hello with their ears. ☐

4 Giraffes don't like sleeping. ☐

5 Giraffes have pink tongues. ☐

6 Giraffes use their tongues to clean their ears. ☐

Lesson 7 Can understand short texts about amazing wild animals

18 Write five facts about a wild animal.

 **PROJECT** 2

1. Lions live in Africa.
2. Their roar is very loud.
3. They can run very fast.
4. They don't like swimming.
5. They can see very well at night.

1 **Think** about an amazing wild animal.
2 **Draw** or print a picture of the animal.
3 **Write** five interesting facts about the animal.
4 **Share** your facts with the class.

Tell your family the facts about your amazing wild animal.

19 Listen.

PHONICS

1    2

20  Listen and blend the sounds.

21 Underline *all* and *aw*. Read the sentences aloud.

1   Don't yawn in class!

2   Draw a red car.

3   My cat has a big claw.

4   The wall is tall and the boy is small.

Lesson 8   Can make a poster about a wild animal / Can pronounce the sounds *all* and *aw*   31

22 Listen and check (✓).

1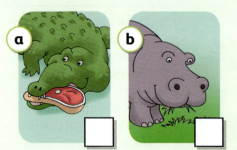

2

3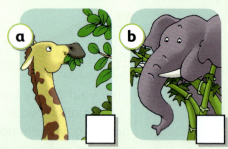

4

23 Write.

1 Do lions eat meat?
   Yes, _____.

2 What do giraffes eat?
   They _____
   _____.

3 Do crocodiles eat fruit?
   No, _____.

4 What do crabs eat?
   They _____
   _____.

24 Choose a picture. Ask and answer.

Where do giraffes live?

They live in grasslands and forests.

I CAN
I can identify wild animals, their food, and where they live.
I can ask and answer about wild animals.
I can understand short texts about amazing wild animals.

Lesson 9

Can assess what I have learned in Unit 2

25   Choose a picture. Ask and answer.

Do they live in the desert?

No, they don't.

Do they eat worms?

Yes, they do.

Do they live in rivers?

Yes, they do...

1. Students play in pairs. Each student chooses an animal without saying the name.
2. Students play rock-paper-scissors. The winner is the first one to ask about his/her classmate's animal and guess correctly.
3. Students take turns asking and answering. Each student is allowed to ask three questions before guessing the animal. This is a timed activity – the student with the most correct guesses when the time is over wins.

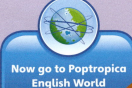

Now go to Poptropica English World

Lesson 10

Can use what I have learned in Unit 2

33

Review Units 1 and 2

1 Listen and number. Then ask and answer.

> Picture a. What does she like doing?

> She likes skiing.

2 What do they like doing? Write.

1 She _____. 2 They _____.

3 _____ 4 _____

34 Review — Can talk about free-time activities

3 Listen and number.

4 Write T = True or F = False. Then listen and check.

1   Elephants live in deserts.
2   They eat leaves and grass.
3   They have a lot of teeth.
4   Giraffes live in grasslands.
5   They eat worms and insects.
6   They have long pink tongues.

5   Look at Activity 4. Ask and answer.

Where do elephants live?

They live in grasslands.

What do they eat?

They eat leaves and grass.

Review

Can talk about wild animals

35

3 The seasons

1. ⭐ What do you know?
2. 🎧 A:50 Listen and find.

- stormy
- thunder
- lightning
- humid
- wet
- temperature
- degrees

3. 🎧 A:51 Listen and ✓ or ✗.

4. 🎧 A:52 Listen and say.

36 Lesson 1   Can identify some weather words

5 Listen and chant.

What's the weather like today?
It's cloudy and wet. We're sad, we can't play.

What's the weather like today?
It's hot and humid. We're sad, we can't play.

What's the weather like today?
There's thunder and lightning. We're scared, we can't play.

What's the weather like today?
It's hot and sunny. We're happy, let's play!

LOOK!

What's the weather like today?	**It's** wet. **There's** thunder and lightning.
What's the temperature today?	**It's** 25 degrees.

6 Listen and number. Then ask and answer.

What's the weather like today?

It's...

Lesson 2 — Can ask and answer about what the weather's like 37

7 Listen and number. Then say. VOCABULARY

 a — go camping
 b — go water skiing
 c — go hiking
 d — go snowboarding

 e — spring
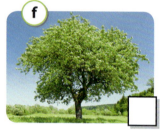 f — summer
 g — fall
 h — winter

8 Listen and circle. Then sing. SONG

Chorus
Spring, summer, fall, and winter
Four seasons in the year. (x2)

It's (spring / fall).
We (go camping / go hiking)
in (spring / fall).
We fish and swim in the river.

Chorus

It's (fall / summer).
I (go hiking / go water skiing)
in (fall / summer).
I jump up high in the sea.

Chorus

It's (summer / fall).
She (goes hiking / goes camping)
in (summer / fall).
She walks and climbs in the mountains.

Chorus

It's (winter / spring).
He (goes water skiing /
goes snowboarding)
in (winter / spring).
He rides and jumps in the (snow / sea).

Chorus

Lesson 3 — Can identify activities you can do in different seasons

I/We/They **go camping** in the spring.
He/She **goes camping** in the spring.

9 Listen and stick. Then say.

1 spring   2 summer   3 winter   4 fall

He goes... in the spring.

10 Listen and read. Then number and write the season.

_____   _____   _____   _____

a It's windy, and I can fly my kite. The weather is cool. There are a lot of apples on the tree in my yard. Yum!

b I like the flowers. The birds sing in the trees. I like listening to the birds and the rain. I love the weather.

c It's hot and humid. Sometimes it's 35 degrees. I go swimming with my friends. I eat a lot of fruit. My favorites are strawberries and peaches.

d It snows, and it's really cold. Some birds don't like the cold, and they fly to hot places. Some animals sleep.

Lesson 4

Can talk about activities and seasons   39

Talk about the pictures. Then listen and read.

  Role-play the story.

13 **Circle.**

1 In the movie, they go (camping / water skiing) in the summer.

2 In picture 2, it's very (cold / hot).

3 In picture 3, it's very (stormy / sunny).

4 In picture 4, it's (hot / cold) and (snowy / humid).

5 In picture 6, Sophie likes the (cold / hot) milk.

14   Write Y = Yes or N = No. Then ask and answer.

Be a good friend.

Me ☐ My friend ☐
Help your friends.

Me ☐ My friend ☐
Make fun of your friends.

Me ☐ My friend ☐
Cheer your friends up.

Me ☐ My friend ☐
Talk badly about your friends.

Me ☐ My friend ☐
Listen to your friends.

Me ☐ My friend ☐
Lie to your friends.

Do you help your friends?

Yes, I do.

Lesson 6 Can understand details of a story / Can talk about being a good friend

15 What do you know?

16 Listen and read. Then write T = True or F = False.

HURRICANE

Do you like hurricanes?
This man likes hurricanes. He's flying into a hurricane with his camera.

What is a hurricane?
A hurricane is a big storm. There's a lot of wind and rain. The hurricane goes around in a big circle. It can knock down trees and houses. There are big waves on the ocean, too.

What's the eye of a hurricane?
The eye is the center of the hurricane. It isn't windy there.

When and where are there hurricanes?
There are hurricanes in the summer and the fall. In North and Central America, they are "hurricanes," but in Asia, the name for these big storms is "typhoons." And in Australia, the name is "cyclones."

1 The man with the camera likes storms. ☐

2 It's sunny when a hurricane comes. ☐

3 A hurricane makes big waves in the ocean. ☐

4 It's windy and rainy in the eye of a hurricane. ☐

5 In Asia, they use "typhoon" and not "hurricane." ☐

17 Write. Then listen and check your answers.

> lightning   storm   temperature   weather

1 This is a _____ warning.

2 The _____ today will be very windy and rainy.

3 There will be thunder and _____.

4 The _____ will be 18 degrees.

42 Lesson 7   Can understand a text about hurricanes

18 Make a mini-book about a natural disaster.

1 **Think** about a natural disaster.
2 **Fold** a piece of paper to make a mini-book. Draw or stick pictures in your book.
3 **Write** about the natural disaster in your book.
4 **Share** your ideas with the class.

Show your family your mini-book. Tell them about the natural disaster.

19  Listen.

1  n**ew**

2  f**ly**

20  Listen and blend the sounds.

21 Underline *ew* and *y*. Read the sentences aloud.

1 There is dew on the grass.
2 I am trying to fly!
3 Chew the stew.
4 My new jet can fly in the sky.

Lesson 8

22 Listen and check (✓).

1   a    b    c
2   a 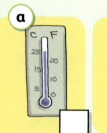   b    c

3   a    b    c
4   a    b

23 Write.

1  Do they go snowboarding in the _____? Yes, they do.

2  _____ _____ in the spring? Yes, they do.

3 She _____ in the fall.

4  He _____ _____.

24 Choose a picture. Ask and answer.

Picture 1b. What's the weather like?   It's wet.

I can identify some weather words.
I can talk about activities and seasons.
I can understand a text about hurricanes.

44   Lesson 9   Can assess what I have learned in Unit 3

25 Write. Then play.

HAVE FUN 3

	Spring	Summer	Fall	Winter
Me				
My friend	☐	☐	☐	☐

Summer. You go swimming.

No, my turn.

How to play

1. Students work in pairs. Each student writes the name of an activity in his/her spaces and his/her friend's spaces.

2. Students play rock-paper-scissors. The winner is the first one to try to guess his/her friend's activities. If he/she guesses correctly, he/she puts a ✓ in his/her friend's space.

3. Students take turns guessing. Each student is allowed to make one guess for each activity. The student with more correct guesses wins.

Now go to Poptropica English World

Lesson 10   Can use what I have learned in Unit 3   45

Wider World 2

Wildlife parks

1 What do you know?

2 Listen and read.

I'm Surian. I live in Borneo. There is an orangutan center near my house. Baby orangutans are cute. They drink milk and eat bananas every day. Orangutans have long red hair and long arms. They live in rain forests. They like climbing trees.

I'm James. I live in London. I like going to the zoo to see animals. My favorite animals are lions. There are some cute lion cubs, too. They like playing, but they have sharp claws.

3 Read and say the names.

1   He lives in London.

2   They drink milk and eat bananas.

3   They eat the leaves at the top of the trees.

4   They have sharp claws.

5   His house is near an orangutan center.

46   Wider World 2   Can understand texts about wildlife parks

I'm Akeyo. I live in the Serengeti National Park in Kenya. The sun shines every day here, and it's very hot. There are a lot of different animals in the park. I like the giraffes. They're tall, and they have very long necks. They eat the leaves off the tops of the trees.

4 Write.

1 Where do orangutans live? They live in _____.

2 What do baby orangutans eat? They eat _____.

3 What does James like doing? He likes _____.

4 Where does Akeyo live? She _____.

5 Which animals does Akeyo like? _____

5 Ask and answer.

1 Is there a zoo near you? Which animals can you see there?

2 Do you go to the zoo with your family?

3 Are there national parks in your country? Where are they?

4 What's your favorite animal? Does it live in your country?

Wider World 2

Can ask and answer about zoos and animals

47

4 My week

1. ⭐ What do you know?

2. 🎧 Listen and find.

3. 🎧 Listen and write T = True or F = False.

4. 🎧 Listen and say.

1

2

3

5

6

7

Lesson 1

learn to cook

do gymnastics

do karate

5 **Listen and chant.**

What do you do on Saturday?
What do you do on Saturday?
I do gymnastics at 10 o'clock.
She does gymnastics at 10 o'clock.
I go swimming at 11 o'clock.
He goes swimming at 11 o'clock.
I have ballet lessons at two o'clock.
She has ballet lessons at two o'clock.
I go skateboarding at four o'clock.
He goes skateboarding at four o'clock.

What	**do** you	**do** on Saturday?	**I have**	music lessons on Saturday.
	does he/she		He/She **has**	music lessons at two o'clock.

6 **Listen and write the time. Then ask and answer.**

1 Oliver has music lessons at _____.

2 Sophie studies English at _____.

3 Phil O'Fax does gymnastics at _____.

4 Finley Keen practices the piano at _____.

4

8

What do you do on Saturday?

I do karate on Saturday.

Lesson 2 Can ask and answer about scheduled activities **49**

7 Listen and number. Then say.

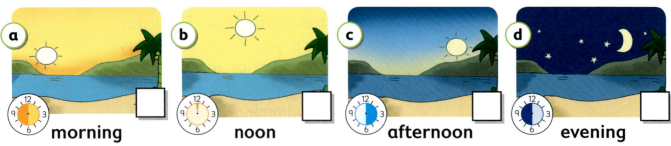

a morning   b noon   c afternoon   d evening

e 2:15 quarter after two

f 2:30 two-thirty

g 2:45 quarter to three

8 Listen and stick or write. Then sing.

When does she study math?
Does she start at ( )?
Does she study math in the
_____?
Please tell me when.
Please tell me when.

She studies math at ( ).
Yes, she studies math at _____.
She doesn't study at _____.
She studies math at _____
In the morning.

When do you learn to cook?
Do you start at ( )?
Do you start to cook in
the _____?
Please tell me when.
Please tell me when.

I start to cook at _____.
Yes, I learn to cook at _____.
No, I don't start at _____.
I learn to cook at _____
In the afternoon.

50   Lesson 3   Can identify times of day and the time

| When | do you | have music lessons? | I **have music lessons** | in the morning. |
| | **does** he/she | | He/She **has music lessons** | at 2:15. at quarter after two. |

9 Write. Then ask and answer.

I _____ on Saturday. I _____ _____ at _____.

I _____ on Sunday. I _____ _____ at _____.

What do you do on Saturday?

I study English.

When do you study English?

I study English at 2:30.

10 Listen and read. Then write T = True or F = False.

READING

What does Fifi do on Saturday?

She has a busy day! She has ballet lessons in the morning. She loves dancing very much!

How does she go to her ballet lesson? Does she walk?

No, she goes by car! She doesn't like walking. Her mom drives her there at quarter to 10.

When does she have ballet lessons?

She has ballet lessons at 10 o'clock.

What does she do in the afternoon?

She goes skateboarding in the park at two o'clock. Then she goes to a party with her friends. She has a lot of fun on Saturday!

1 Fifi has ballet lessons in the afternoon. ☐

2 She has ballet lessons at 10 o'clock. ☐

3 She walks to her ballet lesson. ☐

4 She goes skateboarding in the afternoon. ☐

Lesson 4

11 Talk about the pictures. Then listen and read.

12 Role-play the story.

13 **Read and ✓ or ✗.**

1 Coco has music lessons in the morning. ☐
2 He practices the piano. ☐
3 He doesn't have ballet lessons. ☐
4 He learns to draw. ☐
5 He can't do gymnastics. ☐

14 **Check (✓) three things. Then ask and answer.**

VALUES
Try new things.

Me ☐ My friend ☐
Learn a new language.

Me ☐ My friend ☐
Learn a new instrument.

Me ☐ My friend ☐
Learn self-defense.

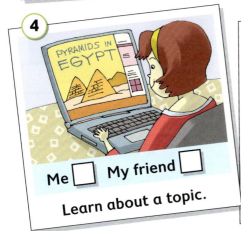

Me ☐ My friend ☐
Learn about a topic.

Me ☐ My friend ☐
Write stories.

Me ☐ My friend ☐
Get a new hobby.

I think writing stories is fun. What about you?

I think getting a new hobby is cool.

Lesson 6

15 What do you know?

16 Listen and read. Then match.

How do you go to school?

1 Lanau doesn't go to school by car. His family doesn't have a car. There aren't many roads where he lives, but there are a lot of rivers. So Lanau and his friends go to school by boat. Their school is on the water, too!

2 Ricky doesn't go to school! His school is very far away. He has classes at home – on the Internet. On Friday, his teacher goes to his house by plane.

3 Susanna lives in a cold place. She doesn't walk to school. She goes to school by snowmobile. She likes riding her snowmobile. It's cool!

a

b

c

TIP!
I go to school **by** boat.
She goes to school **by** snowmobile.

17 Listen and circle T = True or F = False.

1   T / F   2   T / F   3   T / F
4   T / F   5   T / F   6   T / F

54   Lesson 7   Can understand short texts about how other children go to school

18 How does your class go to school? Do a survey.

1 **Ask** your classmates: *How do you go to school?*
2 **Write** down the answers.
3 **Draw** and color a chart to show the results.
4 **Share** the results with the class.

Tell your family about how other children go to school. Show them your chart.

19  Listen.

①  ②

20  Listen and blend the sounds.

21 Underline *ie* and *ue*. Read the sentences aloud.

1 Do you like fried fish?

2 My dad has a blue tie.

3 Is it true that trees are blue?

4 Let's lie on the picnic blanket and eat plum pie.

Lesson 8 Can do a survey on how we go to school / Can pronounce the sounds *ie* and *ue* 55

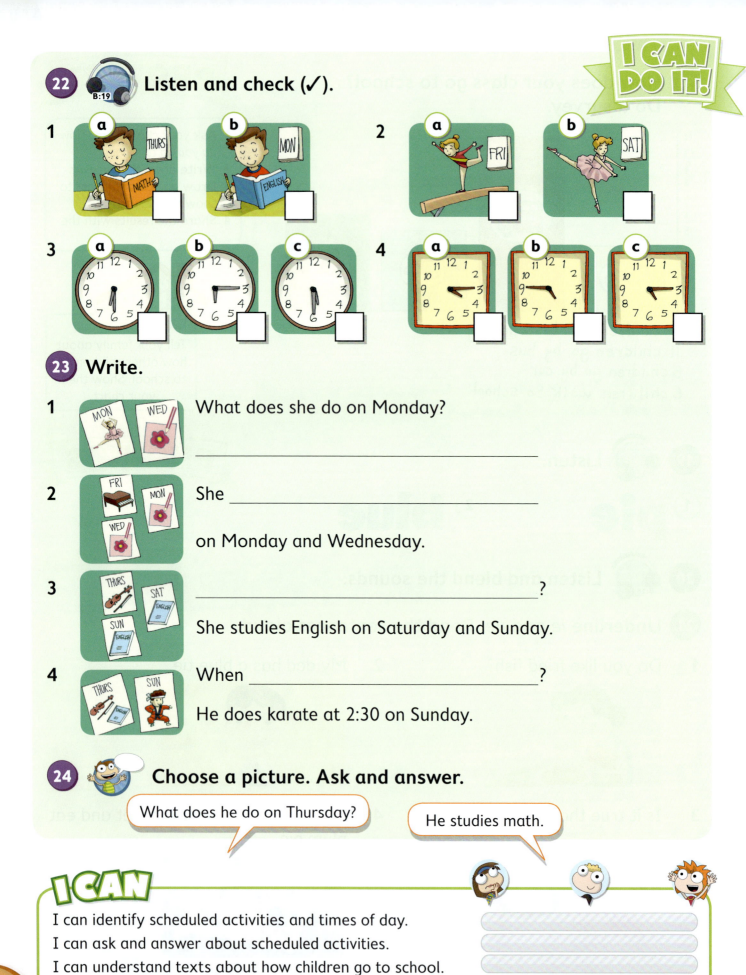

25 Write. Then play.

	Me	My friend
SUN		
MON		
TUES		
WED		
THURS		
FRI		
SAT		

You practice the piano on Monday.

Yes! My turn.

How to play

1. Students work in pairs. Each student writes the name of an activity in his/her spaces and his/her friend's spaces.
2. Students play rock-paper-scissors The winner is the first one to try to guess his/her friend's activities. If he/she guesses correctly, he/she puts a ✓ in his/her friend's space.
3. Students take turns guessing. Each student is allowed to make one guess for each day. The student with more correct guesses wins.

Now go to Poptropica English World

Lesson 10

Can use what I have learned in Unit 4

Review Units 3 and 4

1 Listen and number. Then ask and answer.

Picture a. What's the temperature today?

It's...

2 What's the weather like? Write.

1 There's _____. 2 ☀ It's _____.

3 _____ 4 ☁ _____ 5 ❄ _____

58 Review — Can talk about seasons and activities

3 Listen and number.

 a  b  c  d  e  f

☐ ☐ ☐ ☐ ☐ ☐

4 Listen and check (✓).

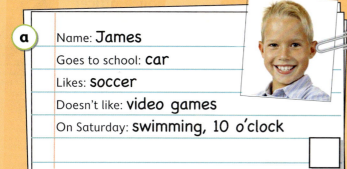

a Name: **James**
Goes to school: **car**
Likes: **soccer**
Doesn't like: **video games**
On Saturday: **swimming, 10 o'clock**

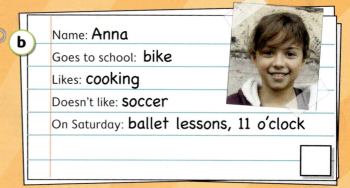

b Name: **Anna**
Goes to school: **bike**
Likes: **cooking**
Doesn't like: **soccer**
On Saturday: **ballet lessons, 11 o'clock**

c Name: **Ben**
Goes to school: **walks**
Likes: **video games**
Doesn't like: **cleaning**
On Saturday: **karate, 10 o'clock**

d Name: **Mia**
Goes to school: **bus**
Likes: **reading**
Doesn't like: **soccer**
On Saturday: **gymnastics, 11 o'clock**

5  Look at Activity 4. Listen and say the names.

6  Look at Activity 4. Ask and answer.

> Let's talk about Anna. What does she do on Saturday?

> She has...

Review — Can talk about scheduled activities — **59**

5 Listen and chant.

What do you want to be? (x2)
I want to be, I want to be,
I want to be a movie star.
I don't want to be a farmer.
I don't want to be a firefighter.
I want to be, I want to be,
I want to be a movie star.
What does he want to be? (x2)
He wants to be, he wants to be,
He wants to be a movie star.

LOOK!

What	do you / does he/she	want to be?	I want / He/She wants	to be	a builder. / an astronaut.
I don't / He/She doesn't		want to be			a builder. / an astronaut.

a photographer

6 Listen and stick. Then ask and answer.

1 2
3 4 5

What does she want to be?

She wants to be a...

Lesson 2

Can ask and answer about what people want to be

61

7 Listen and number. Then say.

VOCABULARY

a. a singer

b. a model

c. a journalist

d. a fashion designer

e. a carpenter

f. a computer programmer

g. a lawyer

h. an athlete

8 Listen and circle. Then sing.

SONG

Chorus
Teacher, farmer, builder, doctor
What does he want to be?
Singer, writer, lawyer, model
Just a minute! Let me see.

Does he want to be a (teacher / lawyer)?
No, no, no. No, no, no, he doesn't.
Does he want to be a (builder / farmer)?
No, no, no. No, no, no, he doesn't.
Does he want to be a (singer / builder)?
No, no, no. No, no, no, he doesn't.
Does he want to be a (doctor / model)?
No, no, no. Yes, yes, yes, he does.
He wants to be a (doctor / model).

Chorus

Lesson 3

Can identify more jobs

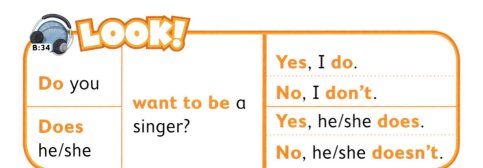

9 Listen and match. Then ask and answer.

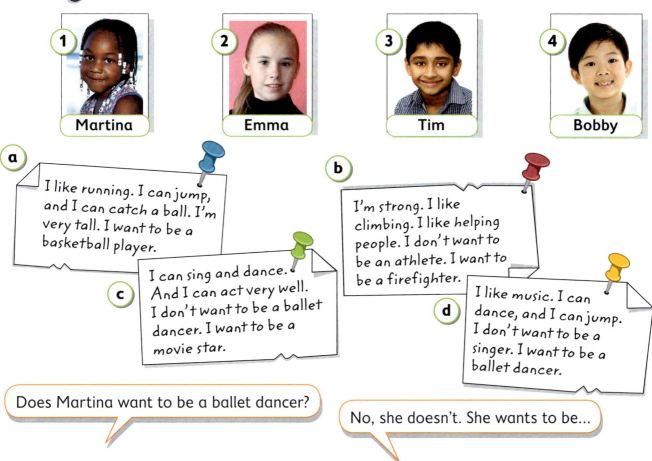

10 Look at Activity 9 and write.

1 What does Martina want to be? _____

2 Does Emma want to be a singer? _____

3 Does Tim want to be a firefighter? _____

4 What can Bobby do? _____

5 What does Bobby want to be? _____

Lesson 4   Can ask and answer about what people want to be   63

11 Talk about the pictures. Then listen and read.

12 Role-play the story.

13 Match.

1. The room is
2. Oliver wants to be
3. Sophie wants to be
4. Coco has
5. They are making
6. Coco is
7. Uncle James counts
8. Sophie takes

a. a space movie.
b. a photographer.
c. a picture of Coco.
d. very messy.
e. 5... 4... 3... 2... 1... .
f. a firefighter.
g. an astronaut in the movie.
h. the script.

14   Write. Then ask and answer.

VALUES

Study, do your chores, and have fun!

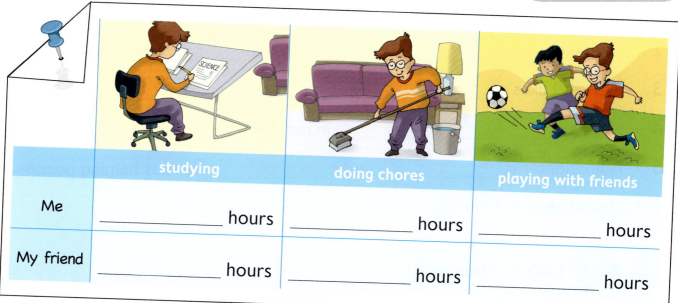

How much time do you spend studying each week?

I study for 10 hours each week.

Lesson 6 — Can understand details of a story / Can talk about the importance of having a balanced life

65

15 What do you know?

16 Listen and read. Then write.

Kids' Forum   POST A REPLY   LOG IN   FAQ

What do you want to be and why? How can you make your dream come true?

Olympian
I want to be an athlete because I want to be famous. I want to be a champion at the Olympic Games. I train very hard and listen to my coach. I eat good food. And I go to bed early every night.

I want to be a journalist because I like telling stories and I like talking to people. I want to be famous. I read a lot and write in my diary every day. I practice speaking aloud every day.
Newsgirl

Flamefighter
I want to be a firefighter because I'm brave and strong. I like helping people. I'm taking care of my body. I'm learning karate to make my body strong.

1   Olympian wants to be a _____ at the Olympics.

2   Olympian _____ very hard and _____ early.

3   Newsgirl likes _____ and _____.

4   Newsgirl _____ in her diary every day.

5   Flamefighter is _____ and _____. He likes helping people.

6   Flamefighter is learning _____.

17 Listen. Then write.

1   What does Julie want to be? She wants to be a _____.

2   Why does she want to be a _____? Because she likes _____.

3   How can she make her dream come true? She _____ hard.

66   Lesson 7   Can understand short texts about what other children want to be

18 Make a collage about your dream job. Ask and answer.

1 **Think** about what you want to be.
2 **Make** a collage about your dream job.
3 **Talk** about your dream job with a classmate.
4 **Share** your ideas with the class.

"Why do you want to be a fashion designer?"
"Because I love clothes."

"What do you do?"
"I am learning to draw, and I read fashion magazines."

Tell your family what you want to be. Show them your collage.

19  Listen.

1 **jungle**   2 **happy**

20  Listen and blend the sounds.

21 Underline *le* and *y*. Read the sentences aloud.

1 When it is rainy, I feel sad.
2 When it is sunny, I feel happy.
3 We paddle into the jungle.
4 It's funny to tickle the little baby!

Lesson 8   Can make a collage about my dream job / Can pronounce the sounds *le* and *y*   67

22 Listen and check (✓).

1 a  b
2 a  b
3 a  b
4 a  b

23 Write.

1 ✗

Does she want to be a doctor?
No, _____.

2 ✓

Does _____?
Yes, he does.

3 What does he want to be? He _____ mechanic.

4 What _____? I want to be a firefighter.

24 Choose a picture. Ask and answer.

What does he want to be?   He wants to be a builder.

I can identify common jobs.
I can ask and answer about what people want to be.
I can understand texts about what children want to be.

68 Lesson 9   Can assess what I have learned in Unit 5

25 Draw and write. Then play.

HAVE FUN

5

carpenter   journalist   lawyer   model   movie star   photographer   singer

Round 1
My dream job

I want to be _____
_____.

Round 2
_____'s dream job
(name of brother, sister, or friend)

_____ wants to be _____
_____.

Round 1

Do you want to be a singer?

No, I don't.

Round 2

Does he/she want to be a computer programmer?

Yes, he/she does! Good job!

How to play

1. Students work in pairs and play two rounds. Each student draws a picture of his/her dream job and that of his/her brother, sister, cousin, or friend.

2. In Round 1, students try to guess each other's dream jobs. In Round 2, they try to guess the dream job of their partner's friend or family member.

3. Students play rock-paper-scissors. The winner is the first one to ask a question.

4. Students take turns asking a question. Each student is allowed to ask only five questions for each round. The student who makes a correct guess with fewer questions wins.

Now go to Poptropica English World

Lesson 10

Can use what I have learned in Unit 5

69

Wider World 3

My hero

1 What do you know?

2 Listen and read.

Hi! I'm Alejandro. I'm from Spain, and I love playing basketball. I play every week. I want to be a famous basketball player one day. My favorite basketball player is Pau Gasol. He's from Spain, but he plays in the United States. He's cool!

My name is Elena. I'm from Russia, and I want to be a ballet dancer. I go to ballet school, and I have ballet lessons every day. My favorite ballet dancer is Natalia Osipova. She's from Russia, and she's a great dancer.

3 Read and say the names.

Who wants to be...

1 a ballet dancer?   2 a movie star?
3 a basketball player?   4 a soccer player?

70 | Wider World 3 — Can understand texts about other children's heroes

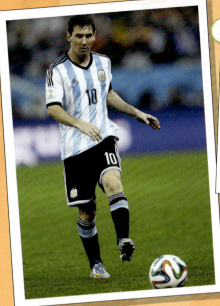

I'm Santiago. I'm from Argentina. I want to be a famous soccer player. My favorite team is Boca Juniors. There are a lot of good soccer players from Argentina. My favorite is Lionel Messi. He can run very fast, and he scores a lot of goals.

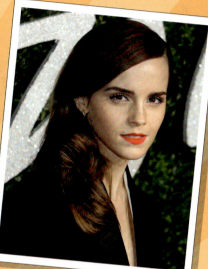

Hello! I'm Kate. I'm from Ireland. I have singing and dancing lessons at school. I want to be a movie star. My favorite star is Emma Watson. She's a very good actor.

4 Write T = True or F = False.

1 Alejandro plays basketball every day. ☐
2 Pau Gasol is from the United States. ☐
3 Elena has ballet lessons every day. ☐
4 Santiago doesn't have a favorite soccer team. ☐
5 Kate doesn't like movie stars. ☐

5  **Work with a friend. Talk about a famous person you admire.**

1 What's his/her name?
2 What does he/she do?
3 Where is he/she from?
4 What can he/she do?

Wider World 3

6 In the rain forest

1. What do you know?

2. Listen and find.

valley

path

bridge

river

3. Listen and write T = True or F = False.

4. Listen and say.

1 2 3

5 6 7

72 Lesson 1

Can identify some places and things in the rain forest

5 Listen and chant.

Where's the gorilla?
It's over the mountain.
Where's the monkey?
It's across the river.
Where's the crocodile?
It's near the river.
Where's Finley Keen?
He's between you and the hut.
No, he isn't. What do you mean?

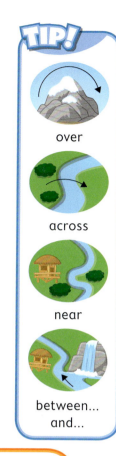

over

across

near

between... and...

 **LOOK!**

Where's the hut?	**It's**	**over** the mountain. **across** the bridge. **near** the waterfall.
Where are the huts?	**They're**	**between** the mountain **and** the river.

6 Listen and number. Then ask and answer.

a

b

c

d

Picture a. Where are the gorillas?

They're... the...

Lesson 2

Can ask and answer about where things are　73

7 **Listen and number. Then say.**

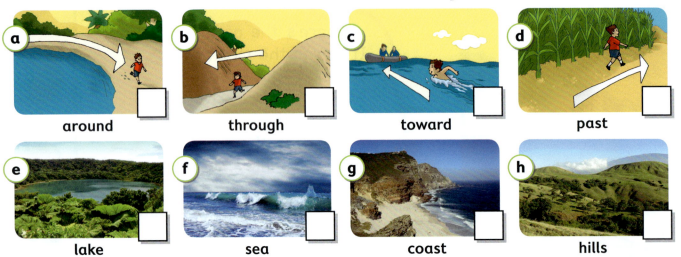

a around
b through
c toward
d past

e lake
f sea
g coast
h hills

8 **Listen and write. Then sing.**

Where are all the gorillas?
Let's watch them eat and play.
They're _____ the hills, across the bridge,
Around the _____ and the trees.

We could walk through the valley,
Climb the _____ and watch them play.
Could I go _____ the gorillas?
Yes, you could, but not so near.

Where are all the gorillas?
Let's watch them eat and play.
They're _____ the hill, next to the huts,
Across the _____.

Could I walk _____ the valley,
Climb the _____, and watch them play?
Yes, you could, but be careful.
You could fall down the hill.

74   Lesson 3   Can identify more places and words that describe direction

 **LOOK!**

| Could you walk around the lake? | Yes, I could. |
| | No, I couldn't. |

I could walk around the lake, but I couldn't swim through it.

9 Listen and write Y = Yes or N = No. Then ask and answer.

Picture 1. Could you swim toward the coast?

..., I...

 1
 2
 3
 4

10 Listen and read. Then write T = True or F = False.

 **READING**

Wednesday, August 20th
Hippos in the lake!
My family and I are sightseeing around Lake Victoria in Uganda. We are staying in a hut near the lake. It's amazing. There are a lot of hippos in the lake. That's why we couldn't swim.

Thursday, August 21st
The Ugandan rain forest
The rain forest in Uganda is amazing.

We couldn't go by tour bus because it's far from Lake Victoria. But we could go by helicopter. We want to go hiking in the rain forest. We want to find the mountain gorillas!

Saturday, August 23rd
Awesome gorillas!
We could hear the gorillas, but we couldn't see them. They walk through the forest and hide from visitors. Suddenly they were there! We could see them from behind the trees.

1 They're staying in a hut near Lake Victoria.

2 They couldn't swim in the lake because of the hippos.

3 They couldn't go by tour bus because the rain forest is far away.

4 Gorillas walk through the grasslands.

5 They could see the gorillas in the end.

Lesson 4 — Can understand texts about places and activities that use could and couldn't

11 Talk about the pictures. Then listen and read.

12 Role-play the story.

13 **Number the sentences in order.**

a   They look at the map.

b   They swing through the waterfall.

c   They find Coco in the cave.

d   They run across the bridge.

e   Oliver sees the monkey near the cave.

14 **Check (✓) the things you need for a hike in the hills. Then ask and answer.**

VALUES

Be prepared.

1	a compass		9	a video game
2	water		10	clothes
3	snacks		11	books
4	a map		12	a cap
5	a phone		13	sunglasses
6	bug spray		14	a ball
7	sunblock		15	medicine
8	a first aid kit			

Do you have a compass?

Yes, I do.

Lesson 6

Can understand details of a story / Can talk about being prepared

77

15   What do you know?

16   Listen and read. Then write T = True or F = False.

The Amazon rain forest

It's hot and humid in the Amazon rain forest, and there are a lot of tall trees. The Amazon River runs through the rain forest. It's very long. A lot of animals live in the rain forest and the river.

hummingbird

These birds are very small. They drink nectar from flowers. They like red, orange, and yellow flowers.

These birds have very long tails. They live in the trees. They have pretty colors. They make a lot of noise.

parrot

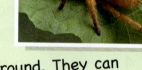

giant tarantula

These big spiders have long legs. They live in holes in the ground. They can eat a bird or a mouse.

tapir

These animals have short necks. They live next to the river. They eat leaves and fruit. They love bananas.

1 It's hot and humid in the Amazon. ☐
2 Parrots have short tails. ☐
3 Parrots are very quiet. ☐
4 Hummingbirds like red, yellow, and orange flowers. ☐
5 Tapirs eat meat. ☐
6 Giant tarantulas live in trees in the rain forest. ☐

17 Make a fact file about a rain forest animal.

1 **Choose** a rain forest animal.
2 **Draw** or find a picture of the animal.
3 **Write** some facts about your animal.
4 **Share** the facts with the class.

Tell your family about your rain forest animal. Show them your fact file.

PHONICS

18 Listen.

1 **center** 2 **ice** 3 **city** 4 **circus**

19 Listen and blend the sounds.

20 Underline *ce*, *ci*, and *cir*. Read the sentences aloud.

1 The prince is eating rice.

2 The princess likes ice in her drink.

3 This is the center of the circle.

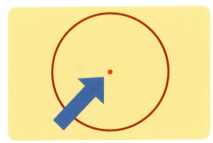

4 The circus is playing in the city for five nights.

Lesson 8 — Can make a fact file about a rain forest animal / Can pronounce the sounds *ce*, *ce*, *ci* and *cir*

21 Listen and check (✓).

1 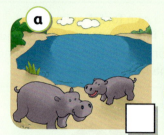 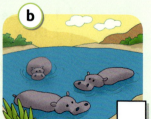 2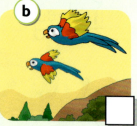

3   4

22 Circle or write.

1  He (could / couldn't) walk through the river.

2 He (could / couldn't) walk through the river.

3 She _____ run over the hill.

4 She _____ over the hill.

23 Choose a picture. Then ask and answer.

Picture 1. Could he walk through the river?

Yes, he could.

I CAN

I can identify some places in the rain forest.
I can ask and answer about where things are.
I can understand a text about the rain forest.

80 Lesson 9   Can assess what I have learned in Unit 6

24 Choose a picture. Then ask and answer.

■ Where is/are…?   ■ Could he/she/it/they… the…?

1

2

3

4
it / swing / Yes

5
fly

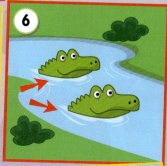
6

7
run

8

9

10
he / walk / No

11

12
walk

Picture 1. Where is the zebra?

It's near the river.

Yes, it is. Your turn!

Picture 5. Could the birds fly past the hills?

Yes, they could.

How to play

1 Students play in pairs.
2 Students play rock-paper-scissors. The winner is the first one to choose a picture and ask his/her classmate about it.
3 Students take turns asking and answering. They only get one chance to answer the question correctly. They get one point for each correct answer. This is a timed activity – the student with the most correct answers when the time is over wins.

Now go to Poptropica English World

Lesson 10 Can use what I have learned in Unit 6 81

Review Units 5 and 6

1 Listen and number. Then ask and answer.

2   **Stick. Then ask and answer.**

Where are the gorillas in your picture?

They're across the bridge. How about you?

3 **Find your way through the maze. Then write.**

1   Could you go around the lake?
    _____

2   Could you go through the forest?
    _____

3   Could you go past the trees?
    _____

4   Could you go around the hut?
    _____

5   Could you go through the waterfall?
    _____

Review

Can talk about where things are

83

yawning

5  Listen and chant.

Why is she smiling?
Because she's happy.
Why is she crying?
Because she's sad.
Why is he yawning?
Because he's tired.
Why is she laughing?
Because it's funny!

LOOK!

Why are you crying?	I'm crying **because** I'm sad.
Why is he/she crying?	He's/She's crying **because** he's/she's sad.

6 Listen and number. Then ask and answer.

angry   happy   sad   scared   tired

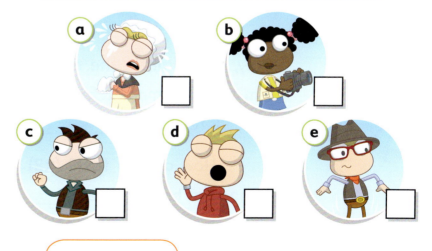

Picture a. Why is she...?

She's... because she's....

Lesson 2

Can ask and answer about feelings using *Why* and *because*   85

7 Listen and number. Then say.

nervous   proud   relieved   surprised

relaxed   embarrassed   worried

8 Listen and write. Then sing.

What makes you feel _____? (x2)
Science tests, science tests, and soccer games
Make me feel _____.

What makes you feel _____? (x2)
High grades, high grades, and winning games
Make me feel _____.

Hey, girl! What's the matter? (x2)
I'm sad. I'm mad, I failed my test.
I feel so _____.

How do you feel? (x2)
I'm fine. I'm happy, I feel _____.
I passed the test.

Lesson 3

Can recognize feelings

LOOK!

What's the matter?	I'm nervous.
How do you feel?	I feel nervous.
What makes you feel nervous?	Tests make me feel nervous.

9 Write. Then ask and answer.

How do you feel?
_____

What makes you feel _____ ?
_____

10 Listen and read. Then write T = True or F = False.

RICKY FANTASTIC

Dear Ricky,
What makes you feel relaxed?
Sam

Hi Sam,
Dancing and singing make me feel relaxed. My friends make me feel relaxed because they make me laugh. We go skateboarding and play video games together. It's fun. What makes you feel relieved?
Ricky

Finishing all my homework makes me feel relieved. Passing a test makes me feel relieved and proud. But I feel surprised when I pass a math test. What makes you feel embarrassed?
Sam

Failing a test makes me feel embarrassed. Sometimes, my mother makes me feel embarrassed. She kisses me and hugs me in front of my friends. Does your mom do that, too?
Ricky

1   Dancing and singing make Ricky feel embarrassed.   ☐

2   Ricky's friends don't make him feel relaxed.   ☐

3   Finishing all his homework makes Sam feel relieved.   ☐

4   Passing a test makes Sam feel proud.   ☐

Lesson 4 Can talk about how you feel and what makes you feel that way   **87**

11 Talk about the pictures. Then listen and read.

12 Role-play the story.

13 **Circle.**

1. The children are in the (Wild West / Dinosaur Park) Studio.

2. Oliver feels (happy / nervous) because he's scared of dinosaurs.

3. He feels (scared / worried) when he hears the dinosaur roar!

4. He feels (embarrassed / relieved) when Uncle James says, "It's not a real dinosaur."

5. Coco is (laughing / shouting) at the end because it's very (exciting / funny)!

Help others in need.

14 **Stick. Then role-play.**

Lesson 6

15 What do you know?

16 Listen to the music and circle. How does it make you feel?

1	scared	nervous	worried	Other: _____
2	relaxed	happy	excited	Other: _____
3	nervous	angry	sad	Other: _____
4	happy	relieved	relaxed	Other: _____

17 Listen and read. Then number.

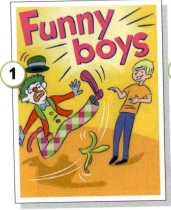  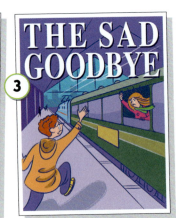 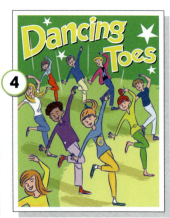

a It's the end of the movie. They're at the railway station. They're friends, and they're saying goodbye. They're crying. It makes me feel sad. It makes me cry, too.

b There are a lot of people. They're laughing. They're learning to dance. The music is great. It makes me feel relaxed and happy. I want to sing and dance.

c There are two boys. They're having a lot of fun. They're funny. They make me laugh.

d There's a big, green monster. The monster has big, sharp teeth. It makes me feel scared. That's why I'm shaking.

90 Lesson 7   Can recognize how music and movies make me feel

18 Make a feelings box.

1. **Find** a shoe box and decorate it.
2. **Collect** things that make you feel happy, sad, excited, scared...
3. **Write** about your feelings. Stick notes on the things.
4. **Share** your feelings box with your class.

HOME SCHOOL LINK

Tell your family about your feelings box. Show them your feelings box.

19 Listen.

1. **gem**   2. **page**   3. **bridge**

20  Listen and blend the sounds.

21 Underline *ge* and *dge*. Read the sentences aloud.

1. The large dog runs under the hedge...

2. ...and over the bridge.

3. Then it runs along the edge of the lake.

4. The gentleman yells, "Gem! Come back!"

Lesson 8

Can make a feelings box / Can pronounce the sounds *ge*, *ge*, and *dge*

91

22 Listen and check (✓).

1 a  b 2 a  b

3 a  b  4 a  b

23 Write.

1  Why _____?

He's shouting because he's angry.

2  How do _____?

I feel worried because I can't find my book.

3 Why are you smiling?

_____ because I'm proud. Look at my prize!

4  What _____?

Going to the beach makes me feel happy.

24 Choose a picture. Ask and answer.

Why is she crying?   She's crying because her friend is leaving.

I CAN

I can identify some actions that show feelings.
I can ask and answer about feelings using *Why* and *because*.
I can recognize how music and movies make me feel.

92 Lesson 9   Can assess what I have learned in Unit 7

25 Play.

HAVE FUN

7

I feel cold and sick.

I'm happy because it's Friday.

I'm tired because it's Monday.

I'm sad because my grades are bad.

I'm worried because I have a test.

I'm excited because it's Christmas.

I'm angry because it's noisy.

I'm happy because it's summer vacation.

I'm nervous because I'm late for school.

Are you crying?

Yes.

Why are you crying?

I'm sad because I can't find my book.

How to play

1. Students play in pairs. Each student chooses a feeling without telling their partner.
2. Students play rock-paper-scissors. The winner is the first one to ask about his/her classmate's feeling and guess correctly.
3. Students take turns miming, asking, and answering questions. Each student is allowed three guesses. This is a timed activity – the student with the most correct guesses when the time is over wins.

Now go to Poptropica English World

Lesson 10

Can use what I have learned in Unit 7

93

Wider World 4

It makes me feel happy

1 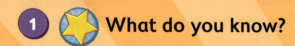 What do you know?

2 Listen and read.

1. lantern

I'm Zhi. I'm from China. Lunar New Year makes me feel happy because it's fun. It's in January or February and it's called the Spring Festival. There are dragons and pretty lanterns. We clean our houses. Then we visit family and friends.

dragon dance

I'm Diego. I'm from Peru. Dancing makes me feel happy because it's good exercise. I dance at a special dance club. Here I am with my friends. We're dancing and wearing traditional dress and hats. Do you like our clothes?

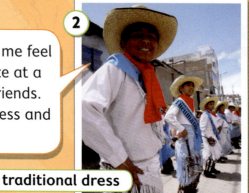

2. traditional dress

fireworks

3.

My name's Mark. I'm from the United Kingdom. Bonfire Night makes me feel happy because it's fun. It's every year in November. I go to watch fireworks at the park with my brother and my mom and dad. I'm not scared of fireworks. In the photo, we're wearing hats and scarves because it's cold.

94 Wider World 4 — Can understand texts about what makes people happy

Hi! I'm Victoria. I go to a special music school, and I sing in the African Children's Choir. At school we have singing and dancing lessons every day. We go by bus and train to other schools and sing in concerts. Singing in the choir makes me feel happy because I love music.

choir

3  **Listen and say the names.**

4 **Write.**

1   When is Lunar New Year?
   _____

2   Why does dancing make Diego feel happy?
   _____

3   Is Mark scared of fireworks?
   _____

4   How does Victoria's choir go to other schools?
   _____

5 **Ask and answer.**

1   What activity or festival makes you happy?
2   When is it?
3   What do you do?
4   What do you wear?
5   Why does it make you happy?

Wider World 4

Can talk about what makes me happy

95

8 By the sea

1 ⭐ What do you know?

2 🎧 C:02 Listen and find.

- a fishing pole
- fishing
- surfing
- a surfboard
- snorkeling
- a snorkel
- a life jacket
- sailing

3 🎧 C:03 Listen and write T = True or F = False.

1. (snorkeling / snorkel)
2. (surfing / surfboard)
3. (sailing / life jacket)
4.
5. (fishing / fishing pole)
6. (horse riding / boots)

4 🎧 C:04 Listen and say.

96 Lesson 1 — Can identify outdoor activities and equipment

kayaking
a paddle

horseback riding
riding boots

4

5 Listen and chant.

Let's go fishing! Great idea!
Let's go sailing! Great idea!
Let's go surfing! No, I'm sorry.
Let's go snorkeling! No, I'm sorry.

I like the beach, and I love the sea,
But sorry, no surfing or snorkeling for me.
I'm scared the sharks will eat me!

Let's go	snorkeling!	Great idea! I love snorkeling.
	kayaking!	Sorry, I don't like kayaking.
Do you have	a snorkel? a paddle?	Yes, I do. / No, I don't.

6 Listen and ✓ or ✗. Then ask and answer.

Let's go...!   Sorry, ...

Lesson 2   Can suggest doing outdoor activities   97

7 Listen and number. Then say.

- a. fond of
- b. crazy about
- c. bored with
- d. scared of
- e. terrified of

- f. rafting
- g. bungee jumping
- h. rock climbing
- i. scuba diving
- j. hang gliding

8 Listen and circle. Then sing.

What are you fond of?
I'm fond of these:
(Sailing / Scuba diving)
and climbing, big rocks, and the sea.

What are you bored with?
I'm bored with these:
(Fishing / Swimming) and sailing.
Not exciting, you see?

What are you scared of?
Being up in the air.
(Bungee jumping / Snorkeling), hang gliding.
Not safe, you see?

Anything else, you ask?
I'm terrified of sharks!

98   Lesson 3

Can identify feelings and extreme sports

 What are you crazy about? | **I'm** crazy about raft**ing**.

9 Stick. Then ask and answer.

crazy about	bored with	fond of	scared of	terrified of

 What are you scared of?

I'm scared of horseback riding.

10 Listen and read. Then write.

Dear Grandma and Grandpa,

I'm having a great vacation at the beach. It's warm and sunny, and there are a lot of exciting things to do. In the morning, I go swimming with dolphins in the sea. In the afternoon, I go snorkeling. I'm crazy about water sports, but Dad says they're dangerous. I'm not scared of scuba diving or sailing.

Mom is bored with swimming. Today she's hang gliding!

Bye!

Tom

Mr. and Mrs. Jones
22 The Street
Greensboro, NC 27401
United States

1   What does Tom do in the morning? _____

2   What does Tom do in the afternoon? _____

3   What is Tom crazy about? _____

4   Is Tom's mom crazy about swimming? _____

Lesson 4 Can ask and answer about doing outdoor activities

11   Talk about the pictures. Then listen and read.

12   Role-play the story.

13 Number the sentences in order.

a   Sophie sees Coco the monkey. ☐

b   The movie director has the script now. ☐

c   Oliver wants to go fishing. ☐

d   Coco wants a banana. ☐

e   Sophie gives a life jacket to Uncle James. ☐

f   Uncle James is sailing the boat. ☐

Enjoy all your activities.

14  Rate from 1 to 6. Then ask and answer.

1 Me ☐ My friend ☐
Reading books and magazines

2 Me ☐ My friend ☐
Going online

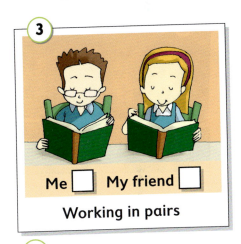

3 Me ☐ My friend ☐
Working in pairs

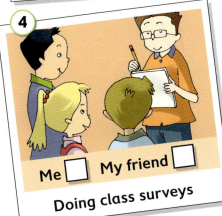

4 Me ☐ My friend ☐
Doing class surveys

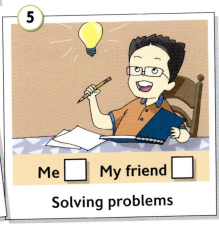

5 Me ☐ My friend ☐
Solving problems

6 Me ☐ My friend ☐
Helping around the classroom

What three school activities are you fond of?

One. I'm fond of doing class surveys. Two. …

Lesson 6   Can understand details of a story / Can talk about enjoying all your activities

15 What do you know?

16 Listen and read. Then write T = True or F = False.

Save the Reefs!

Coral reefs are made of small sea animals and their skeletons. You can find coral reefs in the sea where it's hot and sunny. Coral reefs need sunlight and warm temperatures. They are called the rain forests of the sea because a lot of fish and sea animals live on them. There are seahorses, sea snakes, starfish, butterfly fish, parrotfish, and many more. There are a lot of pretty colors in the reef. How does this coral reef make you feel?

Now look at this coral reef. It's white and there are no fish or sea animals on it. The sea is too hot because of global warming, and the coral is dead. Fish don't like dead coral. How does this coral reef make you feel?

Please help us save the coral reefs.

1 There are coral reefs in cold seas. ☐
2 A lot of fish and sea animals live in coral reefs. ☐
3 There are parrots and butterflies in the reef. ☐
4 Dead coral is white. ☐
5 Fish don't like dead coral. ☐

17 Find the names of five sea animals in the text. Write.

_____ _____ _____ _____ _____

102 Lesson 7

Can understand a text about coral reefs

18 Make a leaflet about protecting nature.

1 **Fold** a piece of paper in half.
2 **Draw** or stick pictures inside and on the back of the leaflet
3 **Write** things we can do to protect nature and a title.
4 **Share** your leaflet with the class.

Tell your family about ways to protect nature. Show them your leaflet.

19 Listen.

1  **ph**one   2  **wh**ite

PHONICS

20  Listen and blend the sounds.

21 Underline *ph* and *wh*. Read the sentences aloud.

1 Can a sheep whisper?

2 Can a whale sing the alphabet song?

3 Can a dolphin talk on the phone?

4 Can a white elephant juggle a wheel?

Lesson 8 — Can make a leaflet about protecting nature / Can pronounce the sounds ph and wh

22 **Listen and check (✓).**

1

2

3

4

23 **Write.**

1  Let's go _____.

Do _____ a fishing pole?

2 What are you crazy about?

I'm _____.

3 Do you have a _____?

_____

4 What are you terrified of?

_____ sharks.

24 **Choose a picture. Ask and answer.**

Are you crazy about snorkeling?

Yes, I am.

I can identify outdoor activities and equipment.
I can ask and answer about doing outdoor activities.
I can understand a text about coral reefs.

25 Write. Then play.

HAVE FUN 8

Me	My friend
Round 1	
Fond of	Crazy about
1 _____	1 _____ ☐
2 _____	2 _____ ☐
3 _____	3 _____ ☐
4 _____	4 _____ ☐
Round 2	
Bored with	Scared of
1 _____	1 _____ ☐
2 _____	2 _____ ☐
3 _____	3 _____ ☐
4 _____	4 _____ ☐

Are you crazy about surfing?

No, I'm not. My turn.

How to play

1 Students work in pairs and play two rounds. Each student writes four activities in his/her spaces and his/her friend's spaces.
2 Students play rock-paper-scissors. The winner is the first one to try to guess his/her friend's activities. If he/she guesses correctly, he/she puts a ✓ in his/her friend's space.
3 Students take turns guessing. This is a timed activity – the student with more correct guesses when the time is over wins.

Now go to Poptropica English World

Lesson 10

Can use what I have learned in Unit 8   105

Review Units 7 and 8

1 Ask and answer.

crying   frowning   laughing
shaking   shouting   smiling

angry   happy   it's funny
nervous   sad   worried

Why is she…?

She's… because….

2 Answer the questions. Then listen and check your answers.

1. Who is Finley Keen?
2. Does Sophie love riding a scooter?
3. Where does Will live?
4. What do hippos eat?
5. What is a hurricane?
6. What does Oliver do on Monday?
7. When does Fifi have ballet lessons?
8. What is Coco in the space movie?
9. What's the weather like in a rain forest?
10. What makes Ricky feel relaxed?
11. What makes Oliver feel nervous?
12. Can you find coral reefs in the mountains?

TIP!
Write your answers on a piece of paper. Count your correct answers.
4 points or under = You can do better.
5–8 points = Good.
9–12 points = You have a good memory!

Review — Can talk about feelings

3 **Listen and number. Then ask and answer.**

What are you terrified of?

I'm terrified of...

4   **Listen and write T = True or F = False.**

Claire, Australia

1. Claire is fond of swimming.
2. She's interested in snorkeling.
3. She isn't scared of sharks.

4. Ryan has music lessons on Saturday in the afternoon.
5. He is crazy about surfing.
6. He doesn't like soccer.

Ryan, Wales

Review

Can talk about how people feel about activities

107

Goodbye

1 Listen and number.

2 Match.

1 Favolina Jolly   a is crazy about skateboarding.

2 Finley Keen   b is yawning because he is very tired.

3 Sophie   c is kayaking with Oliver – they're wearing life jackets.

4 Uncle James   d is eating a banana next to a waterfall.

5 Coco   e is crazy about hiking and camping.

Lesson 1   Can recognize what people are doing

3 Answer the questions.

TIP! Work with a friend. Take turns to answer the questions. Who got the most correct answers?

STORY QUIZ

1 Sophie and Oliver want to… in a movie.	2 Coco takes the… and runs away.	3 Coco likes… 	4 Sophie is… than Coco.
5 True or false: Coco can't jump or climb.	6 What is the giraffe eating?	7 Monkeys eat…	8 What do gorillas love for lunch?
9 Who plays with the weather machine?	10 True or false: Coco can play the piano.	11 Can Coco do gymnastics?	12 What does Oliver want to be?
13 What does Sophie want to be?	14 Does Sophie swing on a rope or a snake?	15 Do they find Coco in a cave or a hut?	16 True or false: Dinosaurs don't make Oliver feel nervous.
17 Is the dinosaur in the story real?	18 True or false: Sophie doesn't like sailing.	19 Do they get the script?	20 Finley Keen's new movie is…

Lesson 2

Can ask and answer about the story

109

4 Stick a picture of your favorite movie star. Write four questions.

1 What is your favorite _____
   _____?
2 _____
   _____
3 _____
   _____
4 _____
   _____

5 Read and stick.

1 The crocodiles are near the river, under the bridge.
2 The monkey is across the bridge in the forest.
3 The hippos are in the river.
4 The parrot is flying past the hut.

6 Write about your favorite animal.

1 What do _____ eat? They eat _____.
2 Where do _____ live? They live in _____.
3 Do _____ like _____? Yes, they do.

7   **Write. Then ask and answer.**

1 What do you like doing? _____

2 What's the weather like today? _____

3 When do you study English? _____

4 What do you want to be? _____

5 What makes you feel nervous? _____

6 What are you crazy about? _____

What do you like doing?

I like painting.

8   **Write. Then ask and answer.**

1 My favorite unit is _____.

2 This unit is my favorite because _____.

3 My favorite part of the story is _____.

4 My favorite project is _____.

5 I like this project because _____.

What's your favorite unit?

It's Unit 3. I like it because it's about the weather.

Lesson 4

Can ask and answer about what I have learned   111

2 **Listen and sing.**

It's Halloween!
It's Halloween!
Don't be scared!
It's so much fun!

The moon is full and bright,
Monsters play tonight.
Witches on their brooms
Fly across the moon.

It's Halloween!
It's Halloween!
Don't be scared!
It's so much fun!

Skeletons move their bones.
Ghosts leave their homes.
Owls go "twit-twoo."
Bats fly to you!

It's Halloween!
It's Halloween!
Don't be scared!
It's so much fun!

A bag full of sweets
Such a great treat!
It's getting late!
Halloween is great!

3 **Look and say *True* or *False*.**
1 The witch is flying across the moon.
2 The skeleton has a broom.
3 The children are scared.
4 The children don't have candy.
5 There are owls.

4 **Ask and answer.**
1 Do you go to Halloween parties?
2 What things can you see at Halloween?
3 How do you dress at Halloween?
4 Do you eat candy and chocolate at Halloween?
5 Do you like Halloween?

Festivals

Can talk about Halloween 113

1 Listen, look, and read.

Pancake Day

In the United Kingdom, many people celebrate Pancake Day. They eat pancakes with sugar and lemon. Some people also have pancake races! They race with pancakes in frying pans. Racers toss the pancakes and try to catch them as they run. It's a very funny race!

2 Read and answer.
1. Where do people celebrate Pancake Day?
2. What do people put on their pancakes?
3. What do some people do on Pancake Day?
4. Do racers carry frying pans?
5. Do they toss the pancakes?

114 **Festivals**

Can talk about Pancake Day

Mother's Day

1 Read.

On Mother's Day we show our moms how much we love them. It's celebrated on different days in different countries, but in most countries it's in the spring.

2 Listen, find, and say.

3 Listen and read.

- breakfast in bed
- rose
- toast
- tea
- box of chocolates

Today is Sunday, and it's Mother's Day. This is my breakfast in bed for my mom. It's a treat because she makes breakfast for me and my dad every day. My mom likes toast and tea for breakfast. Today she has a rose and some presents, too. My present for my mom is a box of chocolates!

4 Read and answer.
1. What day of the week is it?
2. What's Mom having for breakfast?
3. Does she have a rose?
4. Who's giving her a present?
5. What's the present?

Festivals

Can talk about Mother's Day   115

afternoon	p. 50
around	p. 74
(an) astronaut	p. 60
(an) athlete	p. 62

(a) ballet dancer	p. 60
(a) basketball player	p. 60
blushing	p. 84
bored with	p. 98
bridge	p. 72
(a) builder	p. 60
bungee jumping	p. 98

camel	p. 26
(a) carpenter	p. 62
cave	p. 72
chatting online	p. 12
coast	p. 74
(a) computer programmer	p. 62
cooking	p. 12
crab	p. 26
crazy about	p. 98
crocodile	p. 24
crying	p. 84

degrees	p. 36
desert	p. 26
do gymnastics	p. 48
do karate	p. 48

elephant	p. 24
embarrassed	p. 86
evening	p. 50

fall	p. 38
(a) fashion designer	p. 62
(a) firefighter	p. 60
fishing	p. 96
(a) fishing pole	p. 96
fond of	p. 98
forest	p. 26
frowning	p. 84

116 Wordlist

G

giraffe	p. 24
go camping	p. 38
go hiking	p. 38
go snowboarding	p. 38
go water skiing	p. 38
gorilla	p. 26
grass	p. 24
grassland	p. 26

H

hang gliding	p. 98
have ballet lessons	p. 48
have music lessons	p. 48
hills	p. 74
hippo	p. 24
horseback riding	p. 96
humid	p. 36
hut	p. 72

I

J

(a) journalist	p. 62

K

kayaking	p. 96

L

lake	p. 74
laughing	p. 84
(a) lawyer	p. 62
learn to cook	p. 48
learn to draw	p. 48
leaves	p. 24
(a) life jacket	p. 96
lightning	p. 36
lion	p. 24

M

(a) mechanic	p. 60
(a) model	p. 62
monkey	p. 24
morning	p. 50
mountain	p. 72
(a) movie star	p. 60

Wordlist

N

nervous	p. 86
noon	p. 50

O

P

(a) paddle	p. 96
painting	p. 14
panda	p. 26
past	p. 74
path	p. 72
(a) photographer	p. 60
playing video games	p. 12
playing hockey	p. 14
playing the guitar	p. 12
(a) police officer	p. 60
practice the piano	p. 48
practice the violin	p. 48
proud	p. 86

Q

quarter after **two** (**2:15**)	p. 50
quarter to **three** (**2:45**)	p. 50

R

rafting	p. 98
rain forest	p. 26
reading magazines	p. 14
relaxed	p. 86
relieved	p. 86
riding a scooter	p. 14
riding boots	p. 96
river	p. 26
rock climbing	p. 98

S

sailing	p. 96
scared of	p. 98
scuba diving	p. 98
sea	p. 74
shaking	p. 84
shouting	p. 84
(a) singer	p. 62
skateboarding	p. 12
skiing	p. 12
skipping	p. 14
smiling	p. 84
(a) snorkel	p. 96
snorkeling	p. 96
spring	p. 38
stormy	p. 36

study English .... p. 48
study math .... p. 48
summer .... p. 38
(a) surfboard .... p. 96
surfing the Internet .... p. 14
surfing .... p. 96
surprised .... p. 86

T

temperature .... p. 36
terrified of .... p. 98
(two)-thirty (2:30) .... p. 50
through .... p. 74
thunder .... p. 36
toward .... p. 74

U

V

valley .... p. 72

W

walking the dog .... p. 14
warm .... p. 36
watching movies .... p. 14
watching TV .... p. 12
waterfall .... p. 72
wet .... p. 36
winter .... p. 38
worried .... p. 86

X

Y

yawning .... p. 84

Z

zebra .... p. 26

Wordlist

119

Acknowledgments

The Publishers would like to thank the following teachers for their suggestions and comments on this course:

Nurhan Deniz, Alejandra Juarez, Lara Ozer, Cynthia Xu, Basia Zarzycka

Jennifer Dobson, Anabel Higuera Gonzalez, Honorata Klosak, Dr Marianne Nikolov, Regina Ramalho

Asako Abe, JiEun Ahn, Nubia Isabel Albarracín, José Antonio Aranda Fuentes, Juritza Ardila, María del Carmen Ávila Tapia, Ernestina Baena, Marisela Bautista, Carmen Bautista, Norma Verónica Blanco, Suzette Bradford, Rose Brisbane, María Ernestina Bueno Rodríguez, María del Rosario Camargo Gómez, Maira Cantillo, Betsabé Cárdenas, María Cristina Castañeda, Carol Chen, Carrie Chen, Alice Chio, Tina Cho, Vicky Chung, Marcela Correa, Rosalinda Ponce de Leon, Betty Deng, Rhiannon Doherty, Esther Domínguez, Elizabeth Domínguez, Ren Dongmei, Gerardo Fernández, Catherine Gillis, Lois Gu, SoRa Han, Michelle He, María del Carmen Hernández, Suh Heui, Ryan Hillstead, JoJo Hong, Cindy Huang, Mie Inoue, Chiami Inoue, SoYun Jeong, Verónica Jiménez, Qi Jing, Sunshui Jing, Maiko Kainuma, YoungJin Kang, Chisato Kariya, Yoko Kato, Eriko Kawada, Sanae Kawamoto, Sarah Ker, Sheely Ker, Hyomin Kim, Lee Knight, Akiyo Kumazawa, JinJu Lee, Eunchae Lee, Jin-Yi Lee, Sharlene Liao, Yu Ya Link, Marcela Marluchi, Hilda Martínez Rosal, Alejandro Mateos Chávez, Cristina Medina Gómez, Bertha Elsi Méndez, Luz del Carmen Mercado, Ana Morales, Ana Estela Morales, Zita Morales Cruz, Shinano Murata, Junko Nishikawa, Sawako Ogawa, Ikuko Okada, Hiroko Okuno, Tomomi Owaki, Sayil Palacio Trejo, Rosa Lilia Paniagua, MiSook Park, SeonJeong Park, JoonYong Park, María Eugenia Pastrana, Silvia Santana Paulino, Dulce María Pineda, Rosalinda Ponce de León, Liliana Porras, María Elena Portugal, Yazmín Reyes, Diana Rivas Aguilar, Rosa Rivera Espinoza, Nayelli Guadalupe Rivera Martínez, Araceli Rivero Martínez, David Robin, Angélica Rodríguez, Leticia Santacruz Rodríguez, Silvia Santana Paulino, Kate Sato, Cassie Savoie, Mark Savoie, Yuki Scott, Yoshiko Shimoto, Jeehye Shin, MiYoung Song, Lisa Styles, Laura Sutton, Mayumi Tabuchi, Takako Takagi, Miriam Talonia, Yoshiko Tanaka, María Isabel Tenorio, Chioko Terui, José Francisco Trenado, Yasuko Tsujimoto, Elmer Usaguen, Hiroko Usami, Michael Valentine, José Javier Vargas, Nubia Margot Vargas, Guadalupe Vázquez, Norma Velázquez Gutiérrez, Ruth Marina Venegas, María Martha Villegas Rodríguez, Heidi Wang, Tomiko Watanabe, Jamie Wells, Susan Wu, Junko Yamaguchi, Dai Yang, Judy Yao, Yo Yo, Sally Yu, Mary Zhou, Rose Zhuang

Unit 1 Free time
page 15

Unit 3 The seasons
page 39

Unit 4 My week
page 50

morning   afternoon   5:00

Unit 5 Jobs
page 61

Review Units 5 and 6
page 83

Unit 7 Feelings
page 89

Why are you crying?

Relax. Take it easy.

What's the matter?

Don't worry. I can help you study.

Unit 8 By the sea
page 99

Goodbye
page 110